Judy Astley is a self-taught artist, who has exhibited in several London galleries, including the Royal Academy. She has been a successful designer of postcards, greeting cards and clothes. *When One Cat Woke Up* is her first book.

Judy lives with her husband, two children and one cat in Twickenham.

When One Cat Woke Up

For Zelda, Layla,
and Jon

First published in Great Britain in 1990 by
Frances Lincoln Limited, 4 Torriano Mews,
Torriano Avenue, London NW5 2RZ

British Library Cataloguing in Publication Data available on request

ISBN 0-7112-0636-8

Set in Gill Sans

Printed in Hong Kong

3 5 7 9 8 6 4 2

When One Cat Woke Up

A Cat Counting Book

Judy Astley

FRANCES LINCOLN

When one cat
woke up

1

she stole . . .

two fish

2

and fought with . . .

three teddy bears

3

and crumpled . . .

four shirts

4

and broke . . .

five cups

5

and unravelled . . .

six balls of wool

6

and tangled . . .

H
h
b
B
F
f
A
a

seven sheep

and knocked over . . .

eight flowers

8

and frightened . . .

nine frogs

9

and left . . .

10

ten muddy pawprints

on her way back to sleep.

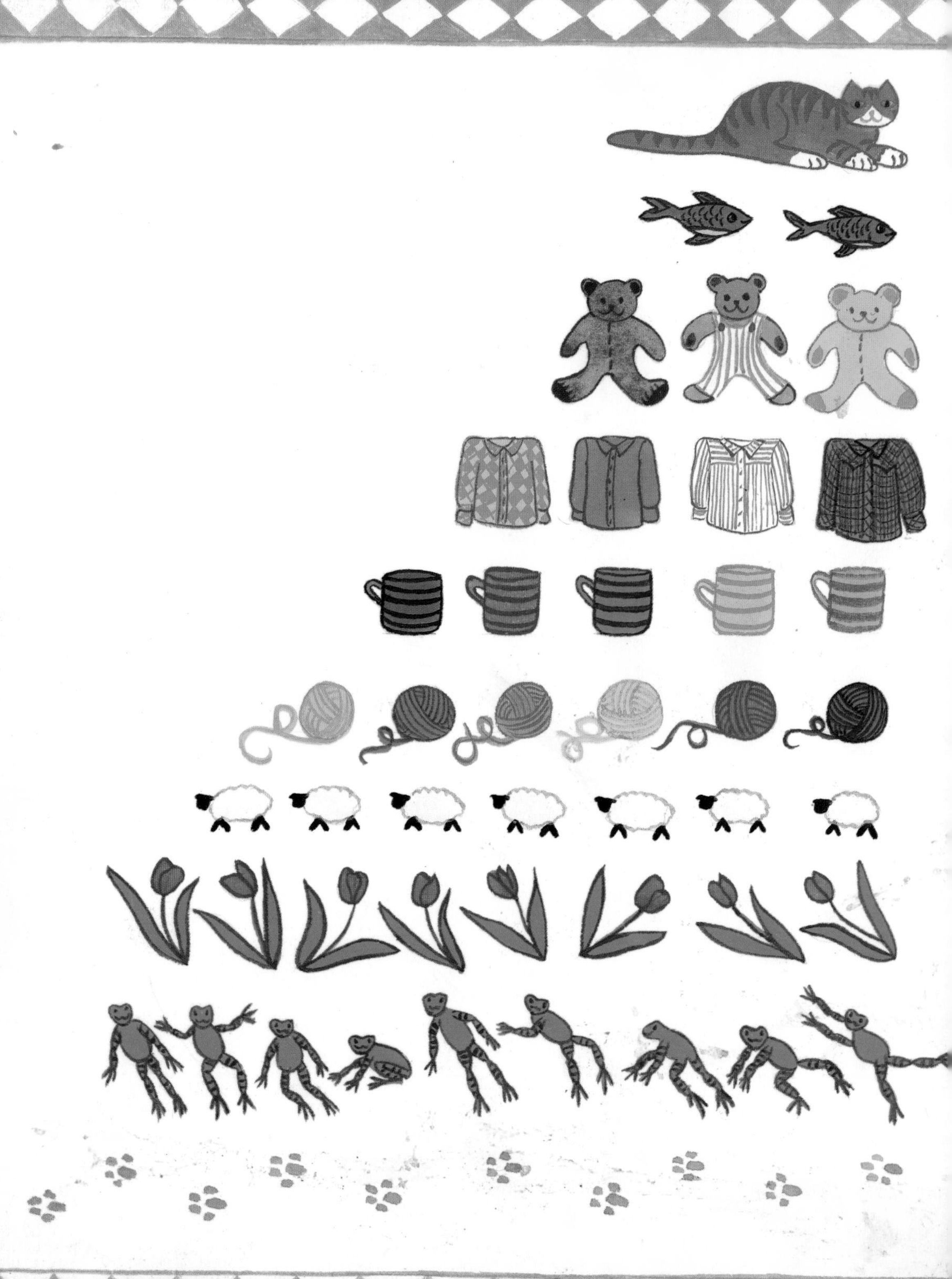

1 cat
2 fish
3 teddy bears
4 shirts
5 cups
6 balls of wool
7 sheep
8 flowers
9 frogs
10 muddy pawprints

OTHER PICTURE BOOKS IN PAPERBACK FROM FRANCES LINCOLN

ANIMAL PARADE

Jakki Wood

Featuring a nose-to-tail march-past of 95 spectacular species, from Aardvark to Zebra. Never has the ABC been such an adventure!

Suitable for National Curriculum English - Reading, Key Stage 1
Scottish Guidelines English Language - Reading, Level A

ISBN 0-7112-0777-1 £4.99

NUMBER PARADE

Jakki Wood

One slow tortoise, five rollicking, rascally racoons . . . Jakki Wood's birds and beasts gain multiples and momentum as the score mounts to 101.

Suitable for Nursery (Counting) and National Curriculum Mathematics, Key Stage 1
Scottish Guidelines Mathematics, Level A

ISBN 0-7112-0905-7 £4.99

FROM SNOWFLAKES TO SANDCASTLES

Annie Owen

From snowflakes to sandcastles, pumpkins to pyjamas, here is a book of words and brightly coloured pictures for every month of the year.

Suitable for National Curriculum English - Speaking and Listening, Key Stage 1
Scottish Guidelines English Language - Talking and Listening, Levels A and B

ISBN 0-7112-1079-9 £4.99